SCHIRMER'S LIBRARY OF MUSICAL CLASSICS

Vol. 2128

SELECTED PIANO MASTERPIECES

EARLY INTERMEDIATE LEVEL

46 Pieces by 18 Composers

ISBN 978-1-4950-8800-1

G. SCHIRMER, Inc.

DISTRIBUTED BY
HAL•LEONARD®

www.schirmer.com
www.halleonard.com

CONTENTS

Minuet
in G Major

Anonymous
BWV Appendix 116

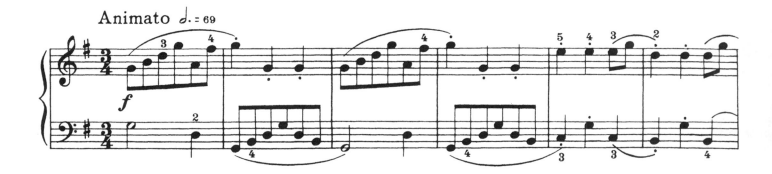

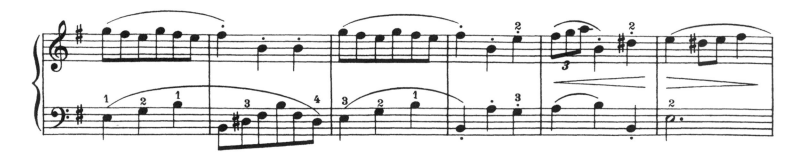

Polonaise
in G minor

Anonymous
BWV Appendix 119

Musette
in D Major

Anonymous
BWV Appendix 126

Allegro con brio ♩ = 112

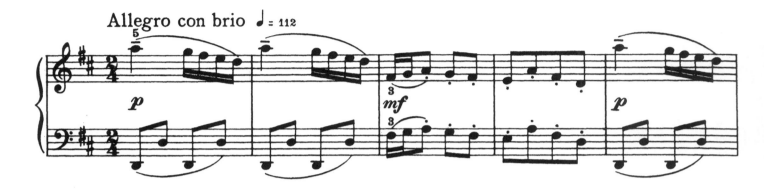

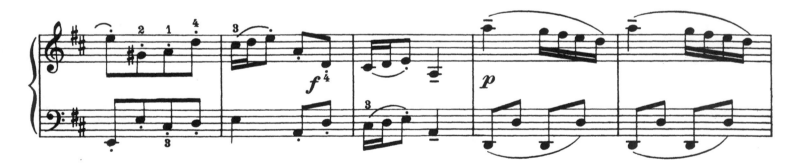

Minuet
in D minor

Anonymous
BWV Appendix 132

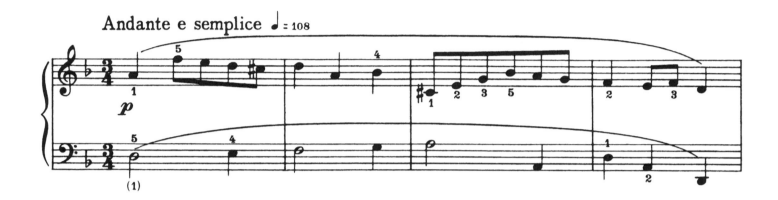

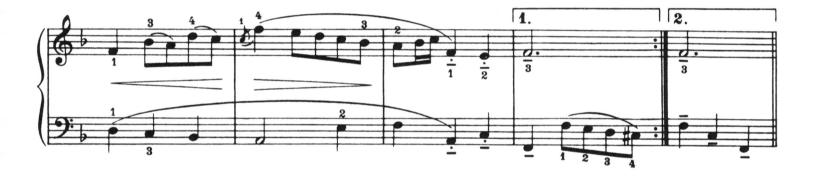

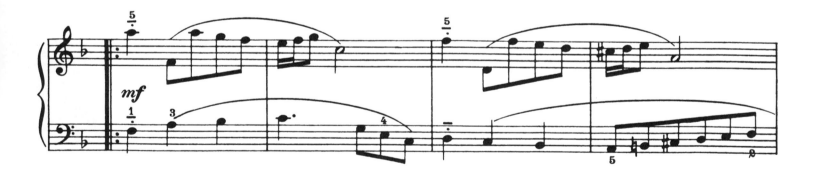

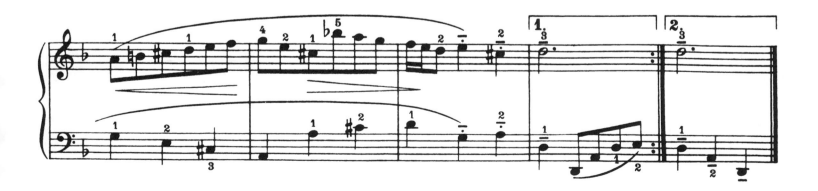

March
in D Major

Carl Philipp Emanuel Bach
BWV Appendix 122

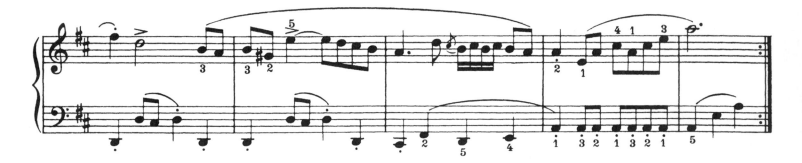

Prelude
in C Major

Johann Sebastian Bach
BWV 939

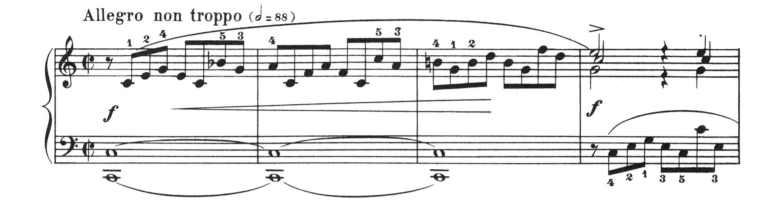

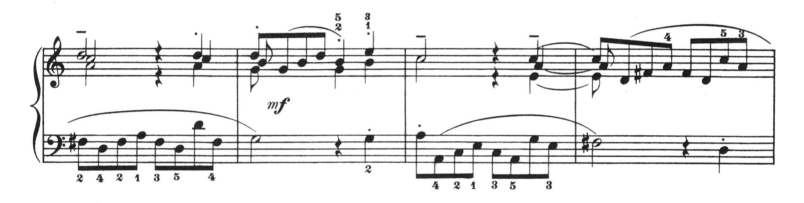

Slovak Youth Dance

from *Ten Easy Pieces*

Béla Bartók

Sonatina
in G Major

Ludwig van Beethoven
Anh. 5, No. 1

Moderato

ROMANZE

Écossaise
in E-flat Major

Ludwig van Beethoven
WoO 86

Waltz
in D Major

Ludwig van Beethoven
WoO 85

La candeur

(Frankness)

from *25 Easy and Progressive Studies*

Johann Friedrich Burgmüller
Op. 100, No. 1

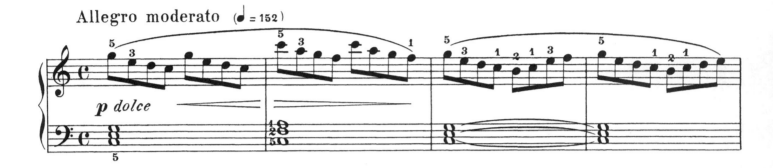

L'arabesque

from *25 Easy and Progressive Studies*

Johann Friedrich Burgmüller
Op. 100, No. 2

Allegro scherzando (♩ = 152)

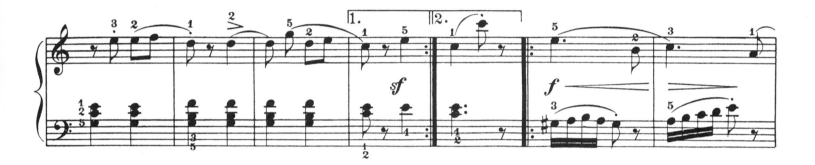

La pastorale

from *25 Easy and Progressive Studies*

Johann Friedrich Burgmüller
Op. 100, No. 3

Andantino (♩. = 66)

p dolce cantabile

cresc.

mf

p dolce

cresc.

p

dim. e poco rall. **pp**

Innocence

from *25 Easy and Progressive Studies*

Johann Friedrich Burgmüller
Op. 100, No. 5

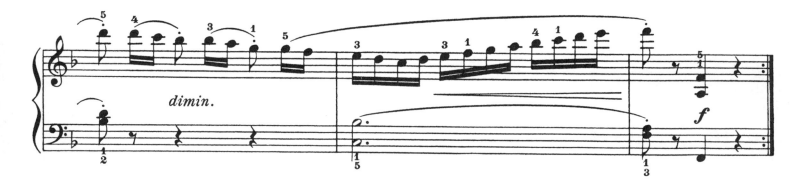

Ballade

from *25 Easy and Progressive Studies*

Johann Friedrich Burgmüller
Op. 100, No. 15

Allegro con brio (♩. = 104)

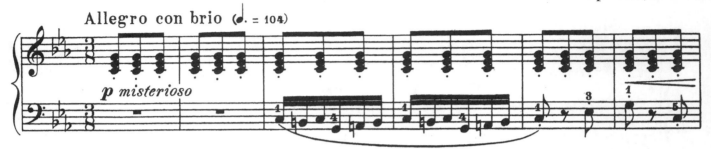

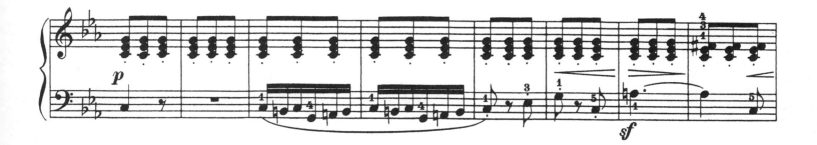

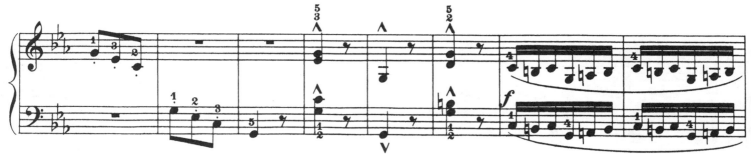

Inquiétude
(Concern)

from *25 Easy and Progressive Studies*

Johann Friedrich Burgmüller
Op. 100, No. 18

Allegro agitato (♩ = 138)

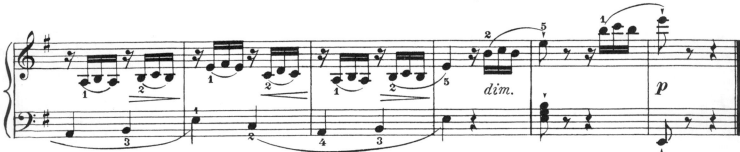

Sonatina
in C Major

Muzio Clementi
Op. 36, No. 1

Spiritoso

Andante

Vivace

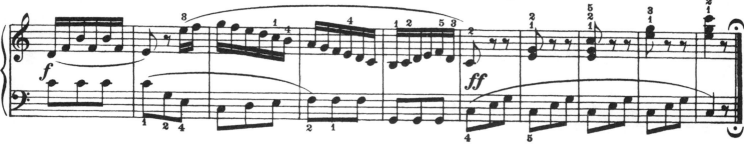

Spinning Song

Albert Ellmenreich
Op. 14, No. 4

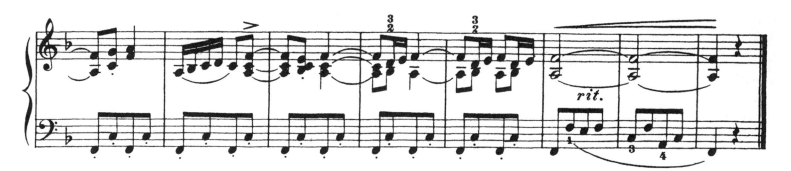

Watchman's Song

from *Lyric Pieces*

Edvard Grieg
Op. 12, No. 3

Molto Andante e semplice

Intermezzo

Sailor's Song

from *Lyric Pieces*

Edvard Grieg
Op. 68, No. 1

Allegro vivace e marcato

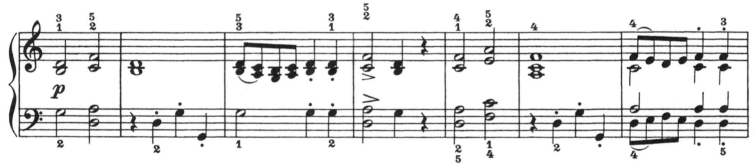

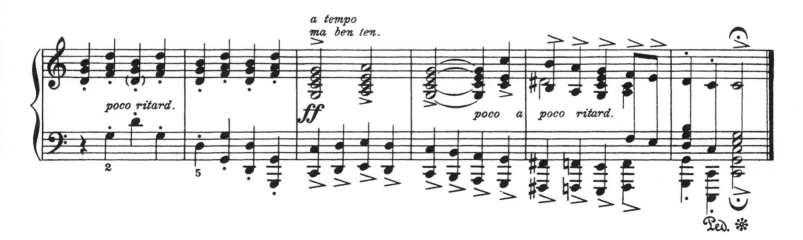

National Song

from *Lyric Pieces*

Edvard Grieg
Op. 12, No. 8

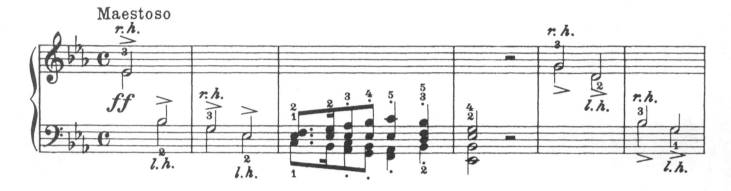

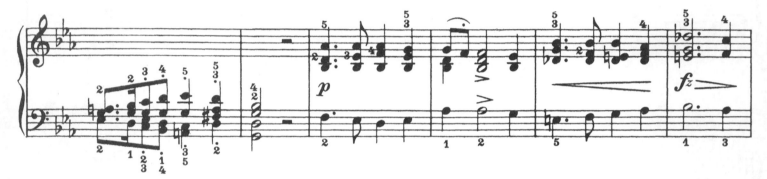

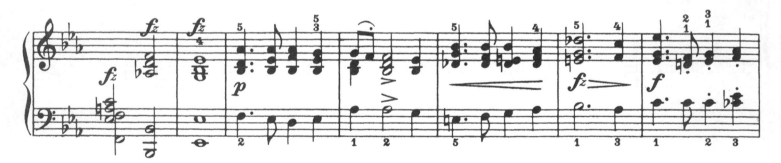

Morning Prayer

from *Albumleaves for the Young*

Cornelius Gurlitt
Op. 101, No. 2

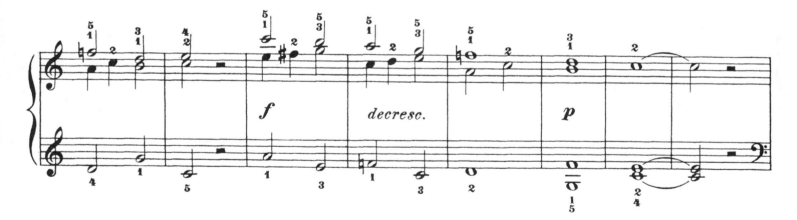

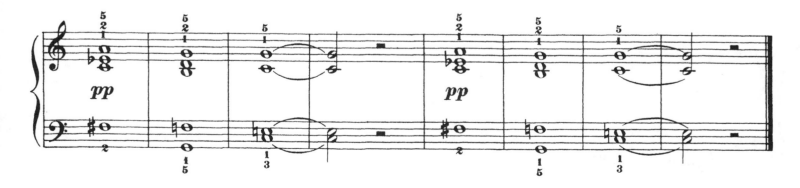

Song without Words

from *Albumleaves for the Young*

Cornelius Gurlitt
Op. 101, No. 10

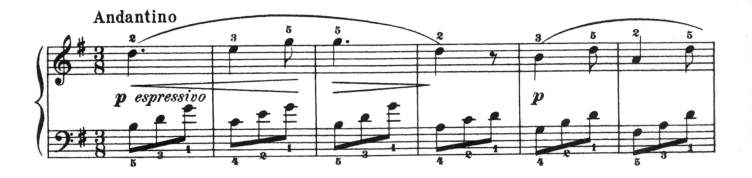

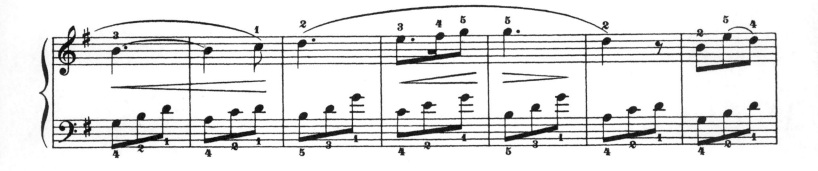

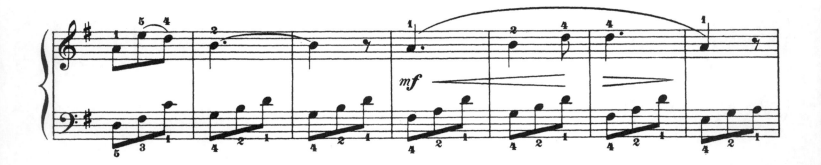

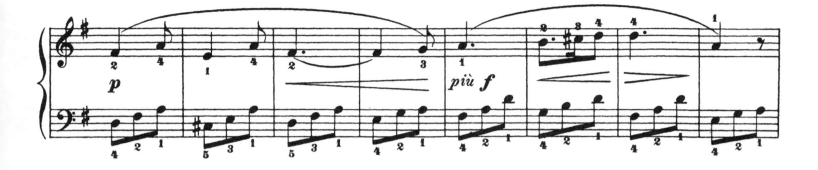

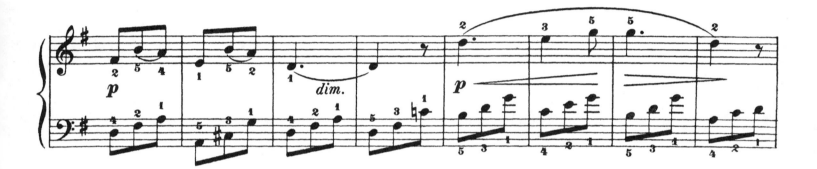

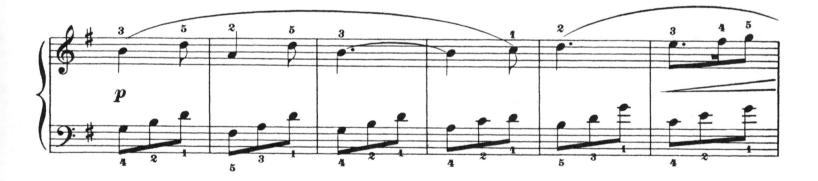

Grandfather's Birthday

from *Albumleaves for the Young*

Cornelius Gurlitt
Op. 101, No. 13

The Clock

from Scenes from Childhood

Theodor Kullak
Op. 62, No. 2

Allegro vivace

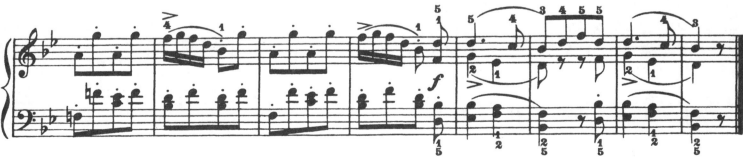

Sarabande

from Suite in D minor

George Frideric Handel
HWV 437

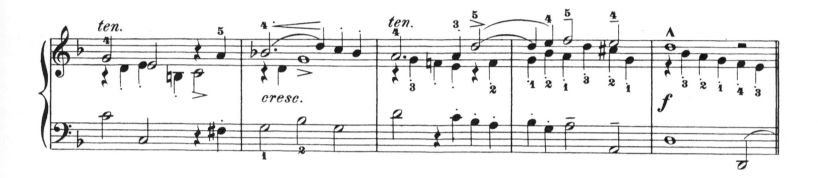

Variazione II

Scampering
from *25 Studies*

Stephen Heller
Op. 47, No. 1

Allegretto (♩ = 80)

Lullaby
from *25 Studies*

Stephen Heller
Op. 47, No. 19

Minuet
in G Major

Christian Petzold
BWV Appendix 114

Minuet
in G minor

Christian Petzold
BWV Appendix 115

Sonatina
in G Major

Carl Reinecke
Op. 136, No. 2

Allegro moderato

Menuetto

Rondino
Vivace

Melodie
(Melody)
from *Album for the Young*

Robert Schumann
Op. 68, No. 1

Soldatenmarsch

(Soldiers' March)

from *Album for the Young*

Robert Schumann
Op. 68, No. 2

Jägerliedchen

(Hunting Song)

from *Album for the Young*

Robert Schumann
Op. 68, No. 7

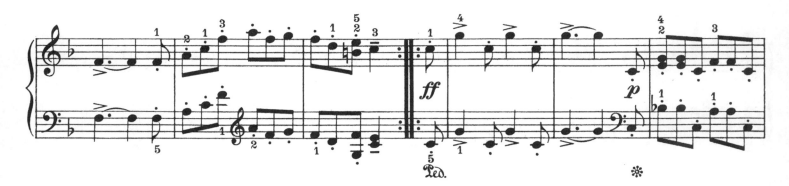

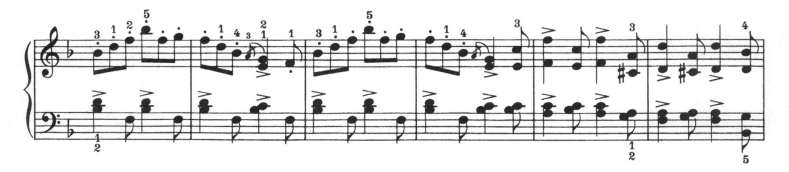

Wilder Reiter
(The Wild Horseman)
from *Album for the Young*

Robert Schumann
Op. 68, No. 8

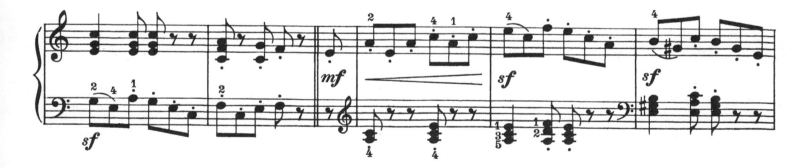

Fröhlicher Landmann von der Arbeit zurükkehrend

(The Happy Farmer Returning from Work)

from *Album for the Young*

Robert Schumann
Op. 68, No. 10

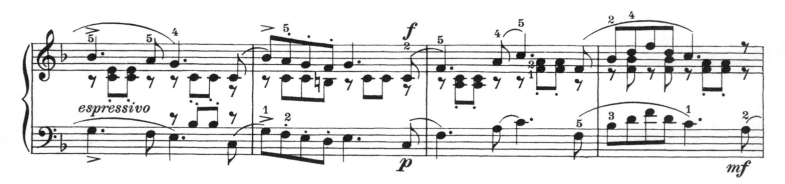

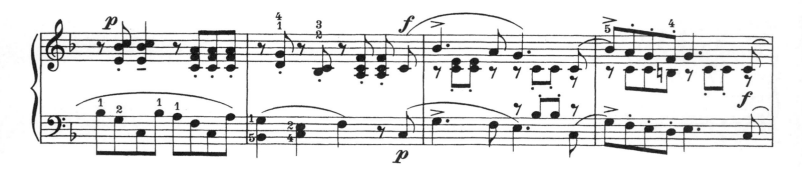

Sicilianisch
(Sicilienne)
from *Album for the Young*

Robert Schumann
Op. 68, No. 11

Fine

D.C. senza repetizione al Fine

Schnitterliedchen
(The Reaper's Song)
from *Album for the Young*

Robert Schumann
Op. 68, No. 18

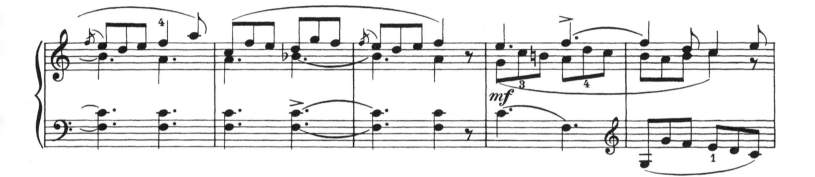

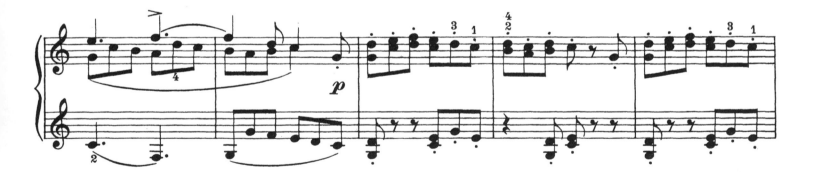

Erster Verlust
(First Loss)

from *Album for the Young*

Robert Schumann
Op. 68, No. 16

Leap-Frog
from *12 Easy and Melodious Studies*

Louis Streabbog
Op. 64, No. 1

Allegro moderato

Jack Frost

from *12 Easy and Melodious Studies*

Louis Streabbog
Op. 64, No. 3

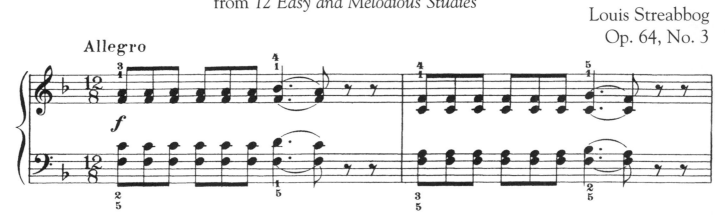

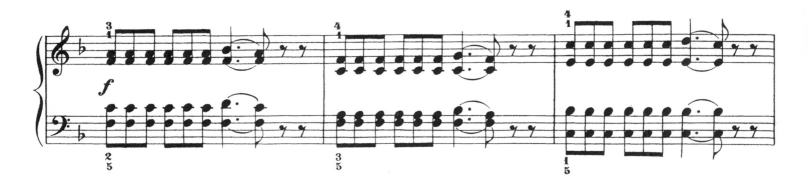

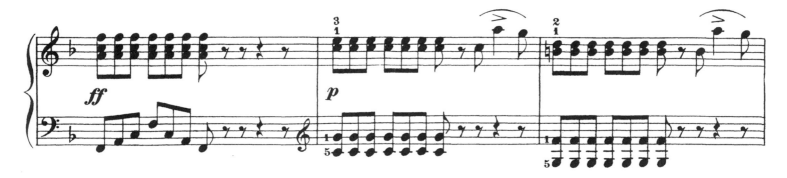

The Woodpecker

from *12 Easy and Melodious Studies*

Louis Streabbog
Op. 64, No. 8

Morning Prayer

from *Album for the Young*

Pyotr Il'yich Tchaikovsky
Op. 39, No. 1

The Sick Doll

from *Album for the Young*

Pyotr Il'yich Tchaikovsky
Op. 39, No. 6

The Doll's Burial

from *Album for the Young*

Pyotr Il'yich Tchaikovsky
Op. 39, No. 7

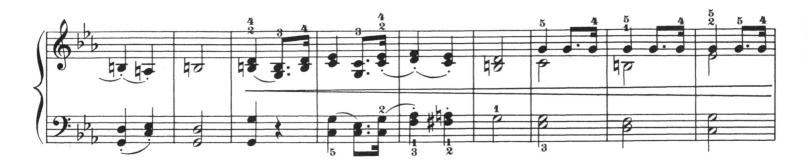

In Church

from *Album for the Young*

Pyotr Il'yich Tchaikovsky
Op. 39, No. 24

Largo

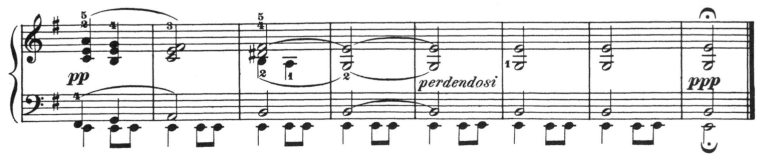